The Adventures of Lizzy and Chuck

Written and Illustrated By

Maria Stanley

ISBN 979-8-89130-968-5 (paperback)
ISBN 979-8-89637-046-8 (hardcover)
ISBN 979-8-89130-969-2 (digital)

Christian Faith Publishing
832 Park Avenue
Meadville, PA 16335
www.christianfaithpublishing.com

Printed in the United States of America

To my children, grandchildren, great-grandchildren, children-in-law, and grandchildren-in-law.

To my son Michael, who is a constant encouragement.

To my daughter Denease, who supports me to improve my life.

To my son Daniel, who called me out of the blue one day and said, "You must get that book published."

And to all who have encouraged me to continue, friends and family alike. You know who you are. You are too many to name here, and besides that, I don't want to get into trouble for missing someone.

Chapter 1

Friends

Elizabeth and Charles lived a long time ago. It was a time long before you and I could remember. They were mostly content with their lives. As rabbits' lives went, they were rather close. In fact, they were best friends. As they were growing up, they talked a lot about leaving the forest. At the rate that rabbits grew, it wouldn't be all that long. Charles had itchy feet as the rumor went. He craved for adventure. He had heard stories that there was a lot more to see than just his little area of the forest. He longed to see if that was true.

Lizzy, as Charles was fond of calling her when he was in one of his teasing moods, did not however have itchy feet. She liked where she lived just fine. She was a little fearful of venturing very far from her familiar surroundings.

God has not given us a spirit of fear, but of love power and a sound mind. (2 Timothy. 1:7)

Charles did not know, and she would not tell him, and that fear kept her homeward bound. She never saw any fear in her mom and dad. After all, they didn't talk about such things as fear. She just didn't want to be known as a scaredy-cat or, in this case, a scaredy-rabbit. Some of her friends looked so timid and shook like willow trees on a windy day every time a human came near. She didn't like seeing that. Besides, Charles was always making fun of the bunnies that were the most easily frightened.

Charles, on the other hand, was one of the bravest rabbits that Elizabeth had ever seen in her short little life. Her father and mother called him reckless and said there was something wrong with Charles. They thought that it was probably due to a lack of proper vegetation. Charles was rather fond of eating things that made other rabbits squirm, such as pine nuts and swamp grass. He said it toughened him up for his future travels. He said if he could eat this stuff, he could eat anything, anytime, anywhere he went. He was probably right. He was almost always trying to get Lizzy to try some of his concoctions. She was generally a good sport and would try some of them.

She knew she could not make a regular diet of them as Charles had done.

One day Charles heard a noise that sounded like pounding. It was coming from the clearing between the two giant oaks at the south end of the forest. He decided to go investigate. It was coming from the area where Noah and his three sons lived. Something was always going on there.

Charles decided to go by and invite Lizzy to go with him. Any excuse to see his friend would do. Elizabeth was in front of her hutch and was eager to go with Chuck. That was her new term of endearment for him—I would venture to say, for him calling her Lizzy.

Give, and it shall be
given unto you.
—Luke 6:38 KJV

Chapter 2

Discovery

Charles or Chuck, as he now preferred to be called, told Lizzy about the noise in the clearing. She agreed that they needed to investigate. After all, it might be one of Noah's boys up to no good.

Noah was well-known in the animal kingdom and well-liked. In the leanest of times and through many a winter, Noah saw that there was feed for the wildlife. Charles never ran out of his kind of food. No one else would eat it. He did like to indulge once in a while in the dried corn and greens that Noah would put out, mostly for the deer.

The animals all thought that Noah was a little strange. Some of them used the term *daft*. He was seen on numerous occasions, walking in the woods and talking to someone that no one else could see. He sometimes called Him Father God or Jehovah. This usually gave the animals quite a lot to talk about.

Elizabeth and Charles got to the clearing just as the sun was getting ready to set. They stayed low in the grass. Noah was up on the side of the strangest contraption the two of them had ever seen.

Lizzy said, "Listen, Chuck. Listen to Noah. He's doing it again."

"What?" said Charles.

"Talking when no one is there," she replied. This time, they heard him asking Father God questions such as, "Where do you want this board to go?" and "Why do you want it so big?"

Charles and Elizabeth never heard a reply. They were quite sure that Noah did because he would nod his head and then put the board in a certain place.

> My sheep hear my voice and that of a stranger they do not follow. (John 10:27 KJV)

Charles was wishing that Noah would ask, "What is this thing anyway?" and that he would hear the reply. Lizzy got so excited because she would have some news to tell the other animals tomorrow. She kind of liked being the first with something new to tell. Charles was very puzzled and very curious. He knew that he would have to find out what this big thing was and what it was for. However, his curiosity would have to wait until tomorrow. He had to take Lizzy home before he got her and himself in trouble. She had to be home before dark.

> Children obey your parents because you belong to the Lord. (Ephesians 6:1 NLT)

As they were walking home, they were so excited that they were both talking at the same time. Neither was listening to the other.

Lizzy said, "I can't wait until tomorrow. I can hardly wait to tell our friends about this and about what that crazy old Noah is up to again."

Chuck was saying, "What was that thing? And Lizzy, did you see how big that contraption is?"

They had one thought in common. They were both thinking that Noah was acting stranger than ever this time.

Neither Chuck nor Lizzy slept very well that night. They were both tossing and turning all night. Lizzy was too excited because she would be the first with news. Chuck couldn't sleep because he was trying to figure out what that big thing could possibly be. Chuck and Lizzy both thought that it took morning a long time to come.

When morning finally did arrive, Lizzy leaped out of bed just as high and as fast as her little rabbit legs would let her. She could not wait to tell all her friends what she had seen and heard the night before.

Chuck decided he had to investigate to find out what the strange structure was. He didn't know where to begin but decided just to hang around close to Noah and his project. *Maybe*, he thought, *I will overhear Noah talking to his sons and will get the answers I want.*

> For there is nothing covered, that shall not be revealed, and hid, that shall not be known. (Matthew 10:26b KJV)

Sure enough just as she thought, Lizzy was very popular that morning. She had, of course, the most exciting story of the week—maybe even of the whole month. She and all her friends decided to help Chuck investigate. You can imagine Chuck's surprise when he was trying to stay low and quiet in the grass, spying on Noah, when Lizzy and her friends showed up. Just to make matters worse, they were all giggling.

Imagine Elizabeth's surprise when she reached the clearing with her friends and noticed the angry look on Charles's face.

"What?" she asked in surprise.

"What, what?" replied Charles sarcastically.

"What is your problem?" asked Elizabeth.

"Nothing," said Charles, and she knew by the look on Charles's face that he was serious and meant business. So they became very, very quiet.

They all lay very still in the tall grass. They were waiting to hear something, anything that would give them a clue as to what that thing Noah was building could be.

> For nothing is secret, that shall not be made manifest; neither any thing hid, that shall not be known and come abroad. (Luke 8:17 KJV)

Noah was by himself that morning. So naturally, he was doing that *thing* again—talking to someone that the animals could not see or hear. Since they all arrived at the clearing at about the same time, they were able to hear the conversation from the beginning this time.

They heard him say, “Good morning, Father,” and “Where do you want me to begin this morning?” They moved in a little closer to hear.

Lizzy’s friends began to get a little nervous about getting caught. They didn’t want to be made into rabbit stew. One of her friends, Sylvia, began to shake like a willow, making the grass around them start to rustle. This made them all more nervous, except Charles, of course. He was just wishing they weren’t there. Then he could be about the business of finding out about this mysterious object.

Charles was listening as hard as he possibly could. He was paying close attention to every word spoken by Noah. It wasn't long before Noah's sons joined him in the clearing. One of his sons asked, "What are you up to now, Dad?"

Noah just replied, "God's business, son."

Charles was anxiously waiting to hear more information about the big object in the clearing of the forest, but it didn't come that day.

They all sat very still in the tall grass for what seemed to be a very long time. It seemed like an eternity to Lizzy and her friends. They were getting very bored and tired of just staying low and quiet. After all, young rabbits were used to running, leaping, and playing. That was just what they wanted to do, go play.

Charles was glad when he heard them start to grumble. He knew they would be gone soon. He could once again be alone to listen for the answer. His curiosity was growing with every minute that he waited for more information.

Lizzy and her friends had decided they had waited long enough. They all took a very informal vote and decided to leave. They figured that Charles was quite capable of finding out about the object and reporting back to them. Charles agreed. After they left, Charles crept up closer to where Noah was working, hoping to hear more about the strange object that was God's business.

Elizabeth and her friends went skipping back to the forest as fast as they could. Sylvia was laughing about Noah talking to someone that they couldn't see. They were all joking about how easily they could have been caught and made into Noah's dinner.

Bunnies like to play different kinds of games with each other. They played leap bunny and jump rope bunny style. The bunnies are very good at both games because they can jump high and do not tire easily. Hide-and-seek was also one of their favorites. Elizabeth and her friends would frolic like this most afternoons.

Because it was getting late and the bunnies were tired, they knew it was time for them to go home to their own hutches. Just as they were all splitting up and heading homes, Charles came running as fast as he could. As you know, bunnies can run very fast. Lizzy could tell that he was very excited by the look on his face and that he was happy about what he knew.

"Lizzy! Lizzy!" Charles shouted "I know what the thing is. I know what it is. My dreams are going to come true. I am finally going to get away from here and see other places. Oh, Lizzy! I really get to see if there are different places outside this forest."

Lizzy's heart was struck with fear. "Charles is leaving, being gone, not here—not here with me." That was all she heard and all she could think about. It made her very sad—very, very, very sad. Something in her heart started to ache, and there was a definite sharp pain right where it was. She started to cry. She started to shake like a willow tree being blown in the wind. Charles was surprised. *Just like a girl,* he thought, *crying when a guy is happy. How can you figure them out?*

Fortunately for Charles, he was smart enough not to speak these thoughts. Instead, he put his paw around her and asked her, "What is the matter, Lizzy?"

Since Lizzy wasn't used to the way she was feeling and didn't know how to explain it to Charles, she replied, "If you don't know, Charles, there is no way I can tell you." Then she turned to leave.

Charles said, "Wait, Elizabeth. Please, can't you tell me why you are crying?"

She answered, "I am not sure why I am crying. It's just that when you said you were leaving the forest, something inside of me began to hurt, really hurt bad. I also began to shake like Sylvia, and you know how much I like that."

Charles immediately understood and said, "Lizzy, I never meant that I would go without you. I couldn't. You are my best friend. You have to go with me."

"What!" screamed Elizabeth. "And leave my hutch and the forest and everyone I know? I can't, Charles. I can't."

Now she was shaking more from the fear of the unknown than anything else, and Charles began to get sad, very sad. What was he going to do? This was what he had always dreamed of—a way to go and see other places and other things. He had to find out if other places even existed and if they were any different than the forest and how. Lizzy's not going, how can that be? A journey—Noah's son Shem called it. Charles knew right away that he had to find out what that was. Now Charles was not only a very curious rabbit with itchy feet but a very sad rabbit who did not know what to do about Lizzy.

Charles's head dropped lower than Elizabeth had ever seen it. He turned and hopped away. *What will I do?* he thought.

Charles and Elizabeth did not see each other for several days. They both hurt too much, and they didn't know what to do.

Thoughts lead on to purpose, purpose leads on to actions, actions form habits, habits decide character, and character fixes our destiny. (Tyron Edwards)

Charles, who liked to think about problems and get them solved, started doing some heavy thinking. Every day he would go to the clearing to hear Noah and the boys talk. Charles did some of his best thinking when Noah was by himself talking to God. After watching Noah solve

problems, Charles decided to give it a try, but he was in no way going to let the others know that he was talking to this God person.

Elizabeth tried to play with her friends, but she missed Charles too much. She wanted to see him but knew that it would hurt. She knew as soon as that big thing was finished, Charles would be gone on his journey.

One day, Lizzy decided to go check out the clearing herself just to see what progress had been made—I think she wanted to see Charles. There he was just like everyone said, lying low in the grass, listening to Noah. Something was different. He wasn't sad, not like she was.

What had happened? she wondered. *Did he have a new best friend?*

She crept up slowly so as not to disturb him. In a soft sweet voice, she said, "Hi, Chuck."

When he saw her, he smiled a big wide smile that seemed to take up his whole face. "Hi Lizzy," he said.

They just sat there next to each other for a long quiet time. Lizzy was the first to speak. "Chuck, you don't seem as sad as the last time that I saw you. What has happened?" she wondered out loud.

"Nothing much, I am just glad to see you, that's all," said Chuck.

> When anxiety was great within me, your consolation brought me joy. (Psalm 94:19 NIV)

"No, I don't think that's it. It is the same kind of look that Noah gets on his face when he is talking to his God friend," said Lizzy.

Chuck just swallowed real hard and said, "Oh!"

Lizzy said, "Yes, and now I want to know what's up."

"We can talk about that later. I want to know if you have changed your mind yet about going with me?" asked Charles.

"No," said Lizzy with anger in her voice. "I haven't, and I think it's stupid and dangerous for you to want to go."

Charles was beginning to feel frustrated, but he stayed calm and replied, "Believe me when I tell you, Lizzy, that it will be far safer on this journey than here in the forest."

"Chuck, do not ask me to do this. I feel safe here in the forest. I am not like you. I don't like adventure. I like boring safety," said Lizzy

> Man cannot discover new oceans unless he has the courage to lose sight of the shore. (Andre Gide)

"Lizzy, listen to me, please," said Charles. "When this thing is finished, Noah and all his family will be on it, along with pairs of every kind of animal. It will leave, and I don't think that it will ever come back. I will be one of the rabbits on it, and I want you to be with me. I must go, and I cannot tell you why. I am asking you to trust me in this. Besides, Lizzy, we are big enough rabbits now to have our own hutch. Since that is what we have always talked about and planned, we might as well do it and be together."

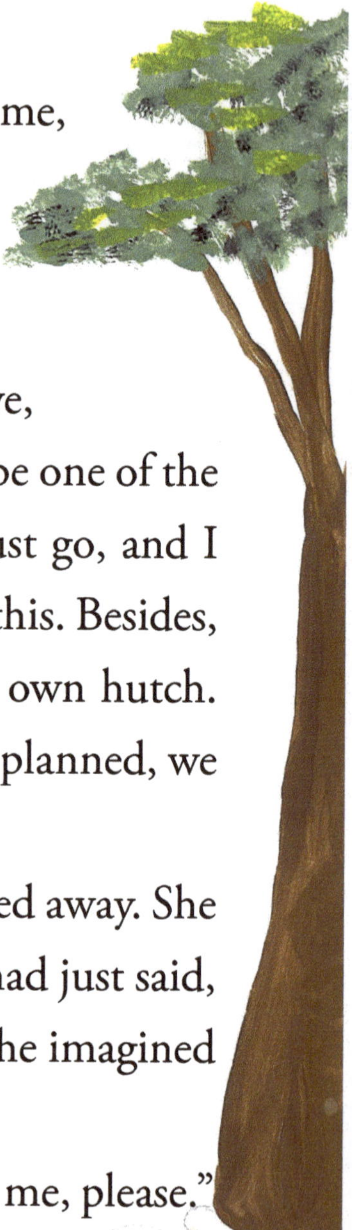

Lizzy just stared at Charles in disbelief and walked away. She couldn't believe what she just heard, what Charles had just said, and how he had said it. This was not the way that she imagined it to be, not at all this way.

Charles hollered after her. "Wait, Lizzy, listen to me, please."

Lizzy just kept hopping away. Charles went after her, hopped right in front of her, and made her look at him. "Lizzy, I know some things about this God that Noah talks to and this ark thing." (He had heard Japheth call it an ark.) "You must listen to me."

"What is it, Charles?" she asked. "What is it that you know?"

"Well, you started to ask me about it earlier. Do you remember?" he asked.

"No," she replied. "Refresh my memory."

"Well, you asked me why I wasn't so sad and that I was like Noah when he was talking to this God friend of his that we can't see. Now do you remember?" he asked.

"Yes, so go on. I'm listening," she said.

"Well, the reason that I have been spending so much time at the clearing was not just to learn about the ark but to find out more about how he knows how to build it and about solving problems. I started noticing that every time Noah

The mouths of the righteous utter wisdom. And their tongues speak what is just. (Psalm 37:30 NIV)

had a problem with the ark, he would stop and talk to his God friend. Then he seemed to know just what to do and he would fix the problem. Have you ever noticed that when he seems to have difficulty with his wife or one of the boys, he goes right to talking to his God friend? Have you ever noticed that he is calmer and has more peace than the other humans we know? Have you ever noticed how Noah doesn't fight with his neighbors like the other humans seem to do?"

Lizzy finally had a chance to reply. Her answer was, "No. I hadn't noticed it before, but now that you mention it, I see that all those things are true of Noah." Almost in the same breath, she asked, "What does that have to do with me getting on that thing you call an ark?"

Call to me and I will answer you, and will tell you great and hidden things that you have not known. (Jeremiah 33:3 NKJV)

Chapter 3

God's New Friends

"I don't know how to tell you this, but I have been talking to Noah's God friend, and He is my friend now too," said Charles. "Lizzy, sometimes God talks directly to me and then sometimes He just lets me know something in my heart."

"Charles," said Lizzy. "Does this mean that our friends are going to think that there is something strange about you like they do Noah?"

"I don't know, Lizzy, and I do not care. But I do care what you think—and more than that I care what my God friend thinks," replied Charles.

"So what are some of the things that this God friend of yours has said?" asked Lizzy.

"One thing that He has told me is that He wants me to be on the ark when it is ready to go. Being on that ark is my purpose in life. He told me that is why I have been eating swamp grass and pine bark all these years and why He made me one of the strongest and bravest rabbits in the forest. I asked my God friend if you

could go with me, and He said that was part of His plan. He said that the choice was up to you and that He would like for you to talk to Him about it yourself. I want you to go with me, Lizzy. But I am still going whether you go or not. I cannot disappoint Him," Charles had said all that he could. The rest was up to Lizzy and her relationship with God.

Elizabeth left in deep thought. "Well, what does Chuck's God friend have that I don't?" Imagine her surprise when she heard a reply.

"Pure unselfish love and peace. Just like I have for you if you will trust me," said Chuck's new friend, God.

Lizzy was in such shock that all she could answer was, "Wow, are you that God guy?"

Silence was all she heard.

Oh, fine, she thought. *Now I am losing it just like Noah and Charles.*

"Trust me, Lizzy," she heard the voice again. The rest of that day, the word *trust* kept going through her mind. When Lizzy got back to the hutch, she had a lot to think about. If she went on the ark, she would have to be very brave like Charles. She would have to leave her parents, but it was about time for that anyway. She would have to leave her friends, but if she didn't go, she would lose her best friend. She would have to leave everything she was familiar with, but if she didn't, she might never see Charles again.

> In quietness and confidence shall be your strength. (Isaiah 30:15 KJV)

"Lizzy," the voice said.

"Yes," she replied, without looking to see who or where the voice was coming from.

"I want you to trust Me and go with Charles."

"Is that you again, Noah and Charles's friend?" asked Elizabeth.

"Yes," was the reply. "I am that I am."

Then He asked her, "Lizzy, have you noticed how you are less afraid of things now?"

"Yes, I think so," she replied.

"Well, that is the way I have made you, to fulfill My plan for your life, for you and Charles's future, and for your benefit," said Noah's friend, God. "I know all things—the past and the future, the beginning and the end—and all my thoughts for you are good. I know how sad you were when you knew that Charles would be leaving, and I know about the time you put the bugs in Sylvia's hutch just to scare her."

"For I know the plans I have for you," says the Lord. "They are plans for good and not for disaster, to give you a future and a hope." (Jeremiah 29:11 NLT)

Lizzy was surprised and ashamed that Noah's God friend knew about the bugs.

"I am sorry about that," said Lizzy. "It won't happen again, I promise."

"I know," said God. "I can tell. Now do you trust me, Lizzy?"

"Yes," said Elizabeth. "Friend of Noah, I will go with Chuck."

"Good," said God. "So will I."

Several more weeks passed, and the ark was finished. Except for loading the supplies and the gathering of the animals, it was complete. The excitement in the forest was mounting more every day as it got closer to loading time. More and more pairs of animals were coming to Lizzy and Chuck and telling them that they were going on the ark with them. Charles noticed a pattern. All the animals that came to him with the same news were the ones that did strange things like he did. They ran in the forest more. They talked of leaving and going to some other place just like he did. They were considered different than their kind.

Charles realized that God did have it all in His control just as Noah had said to his boys the day that Charles overheard him telling them about the rain and the flood that would come. Charles was a little confused. You see, up until this time, there had never been rain on earth.

The day finally arrived. It was time for the loading to begin. First, the supplies were to be loaded. That would take several days. Then the animals would begin to gather. As Charles watched them arrive, he knew that God was drawing each one by His command and He had the whole thing under control. Animals that normally were each other's enemies got along just fine. If they started to get a little excited, Noah would just talk to his friend again, and calm would come over all of them.

Charles believed he was the most excited because he knew beyond a doubt that this was what he had waited for his whole life. It was what he had been trained for. It was his "dream come true." Lizzy was very happy because she would get to be with her best friend for the rest of her life, both of her best friends. Noah's God friend was now her friend also. Charles and Lizzy spent long hours talking to God together and separately. They could talk to Him about everything in their lives and in the lives of their friends that were going on the ark. As a matter of fact, they found out later that all the animals going on the ark knew Noah's friend, God.

They could hardly wait to go aboard.

Chapter 4

All Aboard

As the clouds started slowly rolling over to cover the sun, the sky got dark. Chuck could tell by how some of the animals were stomping around that they were getting anxious to go. Noah could tell also. That was the signal to open the gates and drop the ramp. The animals started boarding. Chuck figured that God told Noah that it was time to get started.

Chuck was so excited that he was jumping all over the place. Bunnies could really jump. He was curious about everything. When were they going to leave? Where were they going? How long would they stay there? Questions, questions, and more questions were running through his mind.

Lizzy was more concerned about meeting some of the other animals on the ark. She was also hoping that they would like her and Chuck. But most of all, she wanted to make some new friends. She was very social, you know.

It took many days for that thing that God and Noah called an ark to be loaded. Chuck and Lizzy were amazed by how many different kinds of animals they saw. There were the animals that they knew from the forest and lots of other animals they had never seen before. It was all very exciting.

Lizzy and Chuck were wondering how they and all the animals were going to fit on the ark. Just about that time, Chuck heard God say, "Don't worry. Trust me. I have it all planned out."

Chuck turned to Lizzy and said, "Don't worry. God has it all planned."

He realized that God had everything planned and he would just rest and wait his turn to go on the ark. Besides, he and Lizzy had a great view of all that was going on.

There were animals of every size, shape, color, and smell. Some were tall, and some short like him and Lizzy. Some of the animals were really huge, and some very tiny, even tinier than he and Lizzy. One thing he noticed, they all had a best friend who looked like them and traveled with them. He again thought that must have been planned by God.

> When you are grateful fear disappears and abundance appears. (Tony Robbins)

Lizzy said to Chuck, “Did you notice that there aren’t any animals that look exactly like us, but there were some that were very similar except for a few changes, like bigger or longer ears?”

“Yep,” said Chuck.

She continued, “I want to meet them all.”

He did not reply.

One thing that came to their attention was that all the animals seemed to get along. Even the ones that normally fought were peaceful to each other. They were all calm and gentle and polite to one another. The big cats were gentle and kind to the deer and other small animals that were sometimes their lunch. The big brown bears were comfortable just walking along with the sheep. The dogs

didn't chase the cats. Even the birds that were usually quite noisy were quiet. They were sure that was God's work also.

All this was noticed by Chuck and caused him to ponder more about what was to come. He knew that going on this journey was about to change his whole life and his world as he knew it.

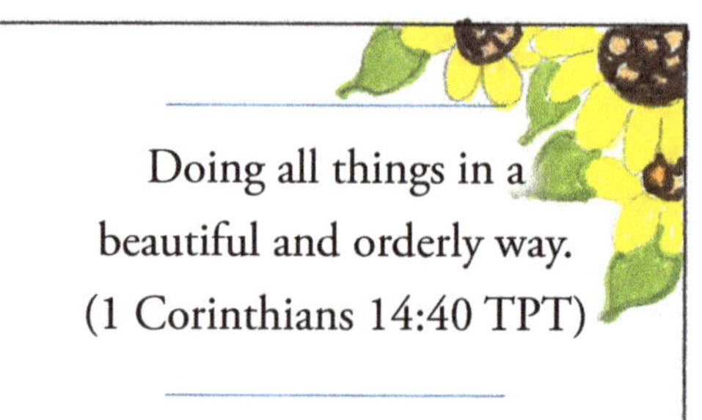

Doing all things in a beautiful and orderly way. (1 Corinthians 14:40 TPT)

Lizzy was aware that there was an order to the loading of the ark, from the largest to the smallest. The largest animals were getting on first. She and Chuck marveled at the giant animal with a huge long nose hanging off of his face. They later discovered that he was called an elephant.

Chuck was quite impressed with what we now call big cats. "You know the lions seem like royalty. They walk like they are in charge of everything."

Lizzy laughed and said, "Maybe they are."

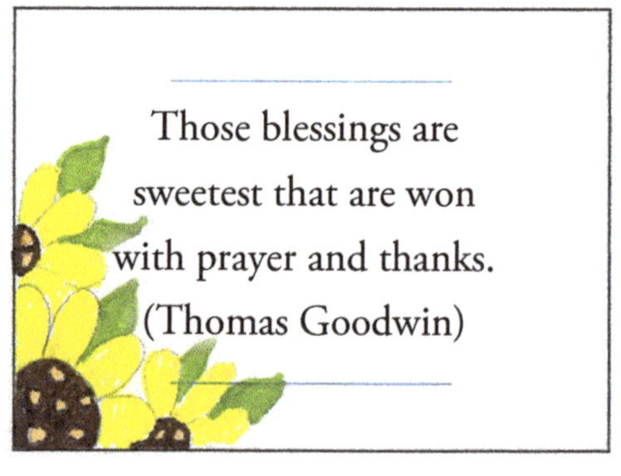

Those blessings are sweetest that are won with prayer and thanks. (Thomas Goodwin)

It was quite a procession, watching them all march up the plank into the opening of that thing that Noah and his boys called the ark.

When it was finally their turn to go on the ark, they were still wondering how and where everyone was going to fit.

The thought crossed Lizzy's mind that Noah's friend,

God, had that all worked out. After all, this was His idea. Up the ramp and into the door they went. Lizzy turned and looked behind her. She was surprised by how many more little animals were following behind her. They were guided by one of Noah's sons to a section of the ark far above the entrance. It was huge and full of rows and rows of little areas with straw. Lizzy assumed it was for the nests.

> You are braver than you believe, stronger than you seem, and smarter than you think. (A. A. Miller)

They settled into an area that felt just right for their needs. They saw some other animals that they recognized. It was actually the whole rabbit and small animal section of the ark.

Lizzy didn't realize that her kind could look so many different ways.

Lizzy and Chuck's little nest was almost in the middle of all the other of their kind. Rabbits of every shape, size, and color were all around her. There were some with really long ears, some with really short ears, some with brown and black spots, or some that were all one color. There were many more small animals, too many to describe. Everywhere she looked there was another rabbit that looked almost like her but not quite.

Water was beginning to fall from the sky, just a little at first. As each day came and went, the falling water increased. This was something of a wonder for all to see because up to this point, the earth had been watered by a fine mist that rose from the earth. Lizzy asked Chuck, with a little fear in her voice, "What is this?"

Chuck replied, "I am not sure about it, but I believe it has everything to do with us being on this ark."

That did not comfort Lizzy. Chuck noticed and said, "We will find out more about it when we are settled."

"Thank you," said Lizzy.

Chuck had what Lizzy thought a very strange look on his face as he was seeing how many different kinds of rabbits there were. Lizzy thought that he looked almost confused. She thought it best to ignore it, and so she did.

By the time the rabbit section was full, they were all exhausted and decided they needed to get some rest. It was dark, and the rain falling softly lulled all the animals into a restful sleep.

Morning came all too quickly. When they awoke, they could still hear the rain falling. It sounded soothing. They were both very hungry and wondering how were they going to eat. They were used to foraging in the woods for greens and such, and Chuck liked his pine needles and bark. This part of the adventure they had not given much thought.

They could hear sounds of the other animals coming from below. Lizzy said they must be the bigger animals because all of them little ones were right here.

Lizzy and Chuck were on the top level with lots of smaller animals roaming around them. Chuck's adventurous side and curiosity started to get the best of him. He wanted to know what the rest of the ark looked like and where were the humans and what were they all doing. He liked watching them.

He turned to Lizzy and said, "Since it was so dark when we got here last night and we didn't get to see much, let's go look around and see what we can find."

As usual little Ms. "Let's Be Careful" didn't want anything to do with the idea. She was afraid that if they got away from their area, they would not find their way back.

She felt warm and safe right where she was. After having a short conversation about what should be done, she decided to stay and meet some of their kind and make new friends.

Chuck didn't much care for that idea. He didn't want to waste any more time talking. He had the whole ark to explore. He told Lizzy, "Do what you like. I'll be back later. If I find something for us to eat, I'll bring it back."

"Okay, have fun," she said. So off he went on one of his many explorations.

Sometimes getting lost is not a waste of time. (Unknown)

As he was hopping away, he thought, *I don't know why she wants to make friends. She has me. And that is all that she needs.* Just then he heard Noah's friend, God, say, "And Me."

Oh yeah, Chuck thought. *Sorry, I forgot you, can read my thoughts too.*

Noah's friend said, "Yes, I know all that there is to know about you."

Chuck thought that this would be a good time to find out about that noise he kept hearing coming from above the ark. It seemed to be getting louder. What was it?

Noah's friend, God, replied, "That is why Noah built the ark to begin with. That is water. It will cover the earth. And all that I have called and chosen to be here will be saved. So enjoy the journey. I have great plans for you."

Lizzy peeked her head over the nest and was gazing around to see what she could. Next to her were some very odd-looking rabbits—odd to her only because they were bigger, fluffier, browner, and had the longest ears she had ever seen on a rabbit.

Lizzy loved and missed her friends from the forest and playing with and making new friends was one of her greatest assets and favorite pastimes. She had lots of fun doing it. So it only stood to reason that she would like to do that here also.

Chapter 5

Abundant Amount of Friends

As Lizzy approached the nest nearest to her, one of the rabbits rose up from a slumbering position. Lizzy could see that this other rabbit was much larger than her or Chuck. In her eyes, this rabbit was huge.

"Yes, what do you want?" said the large rabbit in a very deep stern voice. It took Lizzy by surprise. She didn't expect to feel fear. Just about that same time, the other rabbit that was with this big one rose up quickly and jumped over to where Lizzy was. She spoke in a much friendlier tone and said, "Oh, don't mind him. He just likes to sound that way to scare others. On the inside, he is just a big softy. He thinks that if he is mean when the food comes around, no one will mess with his. I learned a long time ago not to mess with his food. My name is Nancy. What's yours? This guy's name is Brutus. His real name is Barney, but he thinks that Brutus sounds tougher. He changed his name when we found out we were coming on this journey. Do you have someone in your nest with you?"

"Yes," replied Lizzy. "His name is Charles, but I call him Chuck. He is off exploring right now. He shouldn't be too much longer."

Brutus asked Lizzy, "Are you from around here, or did you have to travel from a long way off?"

She replied that she and Chuck were from right where that thing that Noah called an ark was built. "What about you and Nancy?" she asked.

"Oh, we traveled for weeks before we got here. It was a very hard trip. It would have been impossible had it not been for our friend God."

About that time, Brutus took over the conversation. "He gave us food, shelter, and warmth the whole way here. There were times when our very lives were in danger and He hid us." Brutus started getting very excited as he continued, "There was this one specific time, we were coming through a snow-covered valley, and there were some wolves on our trail, sniffing the whole way. He hid us from their sight. They were right next to us and couldn't see us. Yep, He got us here all right. He directed, protected, and provided for us. Knowing Him has been the best thing that ever happened to us."

Lizzy liked what she heard. It made her feel comforted. She decided it was time to go back to her own nest area.

She said, “Goodbye, and it was nice meeting you,” to Brutus and Nancy. “I’ll be back soon.”

Somehow, Chuck had managed to climb down to the second level and see all kinds of animals roaming free and some in cages—some with their gates closed and some with their doors wide open. He was most curious about the cages that were completely covered. His mind couldn't take in all that his eyes could see.

Suddenly, he was very hungry and realized he had been away from his nest area and Lizzy for a long time.

He heard a lot of commotion among the animals and went to look in the direction of the sounds. He saw one of Noah's boys and his wife pulling a big wagon with all kinds of food and passing it out. He also noticed if there was an empty section or cage, they just went right on by and fed the animals.

He started climbing as fast as he could. He made it and found Lizzy right where he had left her. There she was feeding on yummy-looking stuff. He did not care what it was. He just wanted some.

Since he wasn't there, his portion wasn't there. So being the fine bunny that she was, she shared her portion. He was grateful.

Lizzy was full of questions: "What did he see?" 'Was he going out again?" "Did he think that it was hard to find his way around?" and "Would he take her with him next time?"

He was delighted to share with her and to describe to her all the different animals that he had seen. We know them today as lions, tigers, giraffes, monkeys, and many others. That did not include all the reptiles, insects, and birds that he saw.

Do something really nice for someone today and keep it a secret between you and God. (Matthew 6:3–4 NLT)

Lizzy told him about her time with Nancy and Brutus. She left out what Nancy said about Brutus acting mean to keep others away from his food because she wanted Chuck to like Brutus. She asked Chuck if he would go over with her and meet them when they had finished eating. He grunted a little but agreed. They were soon finished, and Lizzy was excited for them to meet.

So over to Nancy and Brutus's nest they went. Lizzy went faster than Chuck did. This time, she was greeted by Nancy. *I think that she must have had a talk with Brutus*, Lizzy thought because as Chuck approached, he was nicer. Lizzy and Nancy should not have been the least bit concerned. Chuck and Brutus got along just great from the first moment they met. In fact, Chuck was wondering why he was so reluctant for Lizzy to meet other friends.

Noah's friend, God, was their common interest. So they spent most of the afternoon talking about God and what He had said to each of them and comparing what and how He had revealed Himself.

Brutus shared how he met God. He was hopping along one day, looking for some parsley or clover. Clover was his favorite to eat, and parsley came in a tight second. Suddenly, he remembered that he knew just where to find some of both.

While he was munching on the clover and getting his fill of the wonderful greens, a human saw him and came running after him with a very large club. Brutus said, "He was angry and determined to do some damage to me. I knew he wanted to turn me into fur trim for something. Suddenly, when the human was right over me, I knew I was a goner. I hollered, 'HELP!'

"I didn't know that I even knew how to do that. The human stopped, turned around, and left. Then I realized I was okay. I started talking right out loud and saying, 'What just happened?'" Then I heard a voice say, 'You asked for help, didn't you?'" Brutus continued, "I was so surprised to actually hear something that I almost fell over. Then I asked, 'Who is that?' then I heard, 'I am that I am.'

“The voice started telling me things about myself that only I knew, and He told me He wanted me to take this journey. And I told Him that I would but would rather not do it alone. Shortly after that, I met Nancy, and He had done pretty much the same thing with her. So now I have a wonderful new friend to share my love of parsley and clover with. Then I was told about His friend, Noah, and this thing called an ark and that He wanted me and Nancy on it.”

Chuck and Lizzy shared the story of how they came to be friends with Noah's friend, God, and what He had done in their lives.

Going to their nest that night had a sweet feeling about it. It gave Chuck and Lizzy much to talk about. They also decided that they had not been spending enough time talking to their friend God. They talked about how they both missed Him and hearing His voice very much. They remembered what Brutus had said, "I talk to my friend 'I am' every day. If I go more than a day or two without talking to Him, I get very nervous and scared about taking this trip and what might be to come."

Brutus said the most important thing that he had learned was all was well when he stayed close to I Am. In fact, every time he got scared or angry or whatever, I Am would say to him, "Barney, [that's my real name] everything is going to be all right."

That night, Chuck and Lizzy went to their own separate little area of the nest. They spent time talking to Noah's friend, I Am, knowing that they were both the same God.

Chuck was very quiet for a long time. He wanted to hear what God had to say to him about his job on the ark. What was his real purpose for being here? Was there anything he needed to do to get prepared for why he was there? The first thing that Chuck heard was, "Thank you for coming and spending time with me." He told Chuck, "I have missed you. I have many things to put into you, and I cannot do it unless you spend time with me and learn to trust in me and what I want to tell you.

"Your only job for now is to spend more time with me, be still before me, and wait on me and what I want to tell you day by day. That is all that I require of you."

Lizzy's time with God was a little different. She wanted to know more about the water coming down, when it was going to stop, and why she was in that ark anyway. Noah's friend, God, was very gentle with her even though her tone was a little demanding.

He asked her, "What are you afraid of, Lizzy?"

"I am not sure what the rest of my life is going to be like. I am not sure that I can do everything right so that you would not leave me helpless."

God was very pleased that she came to Him with who she really was and how she really felt. He said, "I will never leave you nor forsake you. The rest of your life will be just as I have planned if you listen and stay close to me. I am for you and not against you. You are never going to do everything right. That is why you need me. In my kingdom, you will always need me. I planned it that way so that you and all that I have called will learn to trust in who I Am."

Chuck and Lizzy slept well that night. Every night that they spent with Noah's friend, God, on the ark was one of being in His presence and surrounded by His peace.

Chapter 6

Journey Ends

Days on the journey seemed to go quickly. There was much for Lizzy and Chuck to do. Meeting all the new animals was a priority for Lizzy. Chuck still enjoyed watching and listening to Noah, his boys, and the other animals telling their God stories.

A lot of the animals spent much of their time complaining about the journey and wondering why they had to stay inside for so long. They missed their natural surroundings. Some even wanted to go back to where they came from. The ones who were complaining the most were the same ones who didn't talk about their time with God.

Lizzy noticed a pattern in her own life also. When she neglected time with her new friend, God, she was more frightened and lonely and complained more, but in her own mind, not nearly as much as the other animals. She was sure of that.

As for Chuck, he loved hearing a good story to share with Barney, Nancy, and of course, Lizzy. His latest story was always the best.

They were almost always stories about what Noah's friend, his friend, and Barney's friend—I AM (God)—was up to with their fellow ark dwellers' lives.

The latest animals that they visited were the hardest to get to know mostly because they were so big and he was so small. Chuck and Lizzy had a difficult time getting their attention. They were called giraffes. They were the tallest animals on the ark. In fact, they were the tallest that Chuck had ever seen. Their names were Gilbert and Gracie.

As Chuck tells it, it took more courage for him to get to know them than it did to agree to go on this journey. To get their attention, they had to get really close and jump up and down in from of them, then holler as loud as they could. They kept doing it but were concerned that they would get stepped on. It wasn't

Without courage, all other virtues lose their meaning. (Sir Winston Churchill)

until Chuck asked God to help him meet them that Gilbert and Gracie noticed him and Lizzy.

As soon as he was noticed, Chuck spoke up. “Hello, I’m Charles, better known as Chuck. And this is Elizabeth, better known as Lizzy. What are your names?”

Gracie spoke first. “My name is Gracie.”

Then Gilbert interrupted without introducing himself, “Why do you ask?”

Gracie said to Gilbert, “No need for rudeness here.”

He responded quickly, “Gilbert, my name is Gilbert. I apologized for my attitude.”

They both had to bend their necks way down to talk to Chuck and Lizzy. They also had to have a special place on the ark.

Chuck sitting up as high as his body would hold him asked them what their story was and how they came to be on the ark.

Gracie blushed a little and began with, "Well, it is a little embarrassing to tell this story, but since you asked, I'll tell you. In my kingdom, some males mate for life, and some do not. Well, I was being courted by a giraffe by the name of George. He was insistent about being my mate. Then one fine beautiful and bright day, along came Gilbert. They right away started fighting with each other for me. I was so confused as to what to do, to the point that it was causing me to even cry. I was so worried about one of them hurting the other. Giraffes fight by swinging their necks and heads against each other. One day, as I was crying and very upset, I heard a voice say, 'You can stop this nonsense by asking me who you are supposed to be with. I have something planned for you.' I was shocked because I had never heard a voice without someone that I could see before."

I would have fainted had
I not believed to see the
goodness of the Lord in
the land of the living.
(Psalm 27:13 KJV)

Lizzy and Chuck both nodded. They understood.

"My first response was, 'Who are you, and where are you?' Imagine my surprise when I heard, 'I am God, Creator of all. Now I want you to choose Gilbert for your mate.' All I could think of was that George would be so angry and upset. Then God read my mind and said, 'I'll take care of George.'

"I thought good because I liked Gilbert better. Then God said, 'I know that is one of the reasons I chose him.' By the time I found Gilbert to tell him what had happened, he and George were back to being friends and the fighting was over."

Gilbert said, "Yes, that is right, and it was Jehovah who told me to win Gracie as my mate. He also said that He had a plan for us and told me about coming to this ark, how to get here, and that everything would be all right if I would listen and obey. So here we are."

Gracie piped in, "Yes, and He—Jehovah that is—made sure we had everything we needed for the journey. In fact, when He would point out a tree whose leaves were good to eat, they seemed to be the best leaves I had ever tasted. One time, after we were through eating, we continued our journey, and as I looked back, the tree was gone. Jehovah put it there just for us. I am convinced of that. There were several other things that made the trip very interesting. One evening, as we were sleeping, we were awoken by the sound of a lion's roar. When it is just one lion, it isn't usually a worry."

Gilbert interrupted and said, "Yeah, usually just one good kick with these legs and it's a goner."

Gracie continued, "But this time, there were a whole bunch of them, and that can be troublesome."

Gilbert piped in, "I would have liked to see them try anything. One kick from me and it would have been all over."

Seek ye first the kingdom of God and all these things shall be added to you. (Matthew 6:33 KJV)

"Like I was saying," said Gracie, "in a pack, they could be dangerous. But not this time, we put our heads together and prayed and asked God to help us, and all of a sudden, the pride just turned around and walked away. It was as if we disappeared. I think I recognized two of the lions getting on the boat with us."

"What about you two?" said Gilbert. "How did you come about getting on this ark?"

This gave Chuck and Lizzy a chance to tell the whole story of how they watched Noah build the ark and talk to God and learned to listen to Noah's friend, who was their friend now also.

Your Love God is my song, and I'll sing it!... I'll never quit telling the story of your love. (Psalm 89:1 MSG)

They all compared stories about how God knew everything about them, and it amazed them all. Chuck realized he was experiencing a feeling of love and security and safety, knowing that God who seemed to be the all-powerful one knew everything there was to know about him, a tiny little rabbit.

God knowing Chuck's thoughts said, "I know all the birds of the air, and all that moves in the field are mine."

It was getting late, and Chuck could hear Noah's gang coming with the food wagon. He hated missing his feed time. If you weren't at your hutch area, they would just pass you by. He nudged Lizzy and asked, "Are you ready to go?' I can hear the food wagon."

She turned to Gracie and said, "It was so nice to meet you. I'll be back." And off they went as fast as they could to get to their little patch of straw.

Gilbert and Gracie were glad that Chuck and Lizzy decided to go. Their necks were tired of being bent over so far. They spoke of how nice it was to meet more animals and make friends, and they also hoped to have some new friends that were closer to their size. Their dinner came around soon, and then it was time for their prayer time. They liked to do it together. They knew there was a purpose for liking to pray together.

In their prayer time this evening, they decided to ask God for friends who were closer to their size. He suggested they go to another section of the ark. He said he thought that they would be happy with who they would meet.

Gilbert thought that he heard God chuckle a little bit. He heard God say one time that having joy was a very important part of being on this earth, that it would help others to come to know Him. Gilbert was aware that he should work on his attitude so that he could reflect more joy. He came to know that through prayer and talking to Gracie.

> A merry heart does good like medicine. (Proverbs 17:22 KJV)

When Gilbert arose the next morning, he remembered what God had said the night before in answer to his prayer to meet animals more his size. He woke Gracie and said, "Let's get ready to go meet some more animals."

She agreed and swiftly arose, excitedly.

Gilbert said, "Let's pray and ask God where to go to meet them," so they did. God put in both of their hearts the same area of the ark to go. They both shared the thought that this was a different way for God to talk to us.

Then Gracie said, "I'll bet He has a lot more ways of talking to us."

Gilbert gave a little laugh.

Gracie said, "What was that for?"

He replied, "I heard Him say, 'Yep, I sure do.'"

Off they went in His direction.

They didn't know what they were looking for, but then again, God had it all planned out ahead of time for them to meet just who He wanted them to meet. Somehow, they both knew that also. God told them that when you are His, there is a lot of knowledge that you are privileged to have. They began to realize that their new friends were on the same level, which made sense because of their height. They were grateful that they didn't have to travel up to the next level and have to stay bent over for too long. They passed lots of other types of animals. They saw what we call a snow leopard today. And a black leopard was close by. They recognized the lions that were in their camp that night that God saved them. What they had a hard time getting used to was how every animal was so peaceful and kind to each other. There wasn't any type of competition or fighting for space or making another animal their dinner. God knew their thoughts and said to Gilbert, who shared it with Gracie, "There will come a time, a long time from now, when the bear will lay down with the lamb, and it won't be on this ark."

Gilbert and Gracie liked that idea. They were strolling along, and right there in front of them were the animals they were supposed to meet. They just knew it by their size. But they still weren't as tall as Gilbert and Gracie. Gilbert alone was 18 feet tall, and Gracie 15 feet. *But these guys are really big*, thought Gilbert. He has seen them before but never spent time getting to know them. They came from the same part of the world and were in such huge groups that he did not see any need to disturb them or get to know them.

Gracie asked Gilbert, "Why do you think it is so important for us to get to know other animals when we never cared about them before?"

He said, "He would have to give it some thought, and he did."

They walked right up to the big animals and said hello as if they had always known them. The newest acquaintance looked up because Gilbert was still bigger than they were and replied hello back and then added, "What can I do for you?'

Gilbert replied, "Well, Noah's friend,

God, sent us over here to meet you. You are actually an answer to prayer."

"Oh yeah," said the big one. "And how's that?"

Gracie interjected that they had their prayer time and asked God for some new friends more our size. He laughed a little and said, "Well, what we lack in height we make up for in width." And his mate laughed at his joke also, for they were only about 13 feet in height. But Gilbert and Gracie didn't need to bend down as far to talk to them.

Gilbert asked them their names and how they came to be on the ark. The largest of the two said, "My name is Frank, and this is my girl, Wanda." He continued, "As for how did we come to be here? From what I have learned from some of the other animals, our story is much like theirs, except for one thing. The head of our herd's name is Martha, and she came to us one day and told us that God had been talking to her and said that I and Wanda were chosen to go on a trip and that we were to head in a certain direction and God would show up for us. We tried arguing with her, but she is the boss and head of the herd. So we started on our journey.

"We didn't know about God until we started traveling. He just started talking to us one day. The first thing that He told us was, there would be a reward for us one of these days for being so obedient with Martha's instructions even though we didn't know about Him and the ark yet. I was a little scared when He started talking because I couldn't see anyone and I didn't know that those things happened to us animals until we got here and started hearing all the stories of how God directed, protected, and provided for everyone on this trip.

"We always had plenty of water and food, and we didn't have one predator at all, not even a bee. Bees are our most feared enemy. They aren't very big, but they sure can hurt when they sting the eyes and ears or go up our long trunk.

"We were afraid that the journey would be very hard and scary, but as long as we kept talking to God, everything was fine. One day, there was a large gathering of hyenas, and I was concerned for Wanda's and my life. Again, we took our concern to God and asked Him to protect us. We kept walking the way He was directing us, and the hyenas didn't even notice us."

Never be afraid to trust an unknown future
to a known God. (Corrie Ten Boom)

Gilbert and Gracie knew exactly what they were talking about. It seemed to them that every animal that they had met had some story to tell of how Noah's friend, God, rescued them. He either provided food or safety and kept them hidden from predators. He kept them warm in the cold and cool in the heat. He gave them exact directions on how to get to the ark. God even told Chuck that everyone that He had planned to be there had arrived just before He had Noah shut the doors and sealed them up for the journey.

In the meantime, Chuck was out exploring again. He met some animals that were more his size. There were squirrels, mice, moles, rats, minks, beavers, prairie dogs, dogs, and cats.

He was having the time of his life meeting all of them and going back to his nest and telling Lizzy about them. She, of course, was thrilled to hear about each one of them. Some days she wanted him to take her with him to meet them. Today was one of those days. Chuck decided to revisit the mice. Their nest wasn't too far away, and they were friendly and funny.

> All I have seen teaches me to trust the Creator for all I have not seen. (Ralph Waldo Emerson.)

It didn't take Lizzy and Chuck long to get there, and just as he thought, they seemed quite glad to see him. They started giggling just as Lizzy and Chuck approached them. Mark and Maggie were their names, and Chuck introduced them to Lizzy. She responded with, "It is so nice to meet you. Chuck

has told me so much about you and how he enjoys your company." That made Mark laugh out loud.

Chuck noticed that almost everything made Mark laugh. He found humor in almost anything. He said he especially liked scaring humans. He couldn't figure out why they were so frightened of him and Maggie, especially since they were so small and hardly ate anything. Lizzy asked Chuck if he had heard how Mark and Maggie had come to be aboard the ark and what was their story. Chuck replied that he hadn't. Mark and Maggie started telling them almost in unison.

They started off by telling them how they were trapped and put in a cage by the humans, and they knew that they were going to be killed, just like humans did most of the time with mice. They said that they spent the first night in the cage very frightened about what they thought was going to happen the next day. In the middle of the night, they were huddled together for warmth when they both heard a voice say, "If you will trust me, I will get you out of here. I will show you a way to go that will give you much rest and peace if you obey me. And when you get there, I have an important job for you to do." Mark liked the sound of that and said, "Sure."

Maggie said, "Who are you, and where are you?

God replied, "When you get to your destination, you will be told who I am, and I am not visible to you now."

They both replied, "Sure, we will go," for they were almost fearless.

The next thing they knew, they had dozed off to sleep. When suddenly, they felt a jarring and a shaking of the cage. They were startled awake. And the gate was open. They made a fast run for the opening and just barely looked back. They saw one of the humans flat on his face, with his foot stuck right on top of the cage they just left. They knew right away what happened. God had caused the human to trip, which opened the way of escape just as He said He would. They ran as fast as they could, with Mark laughing the whole time. Then as Mark was telling his story, Maggie interrupted him saying, "And just like all the other stories that we have heard about this God, he provided for us, he protected us, and he even understands when we are sad and lonely for our old home."

Many are the plans in a person's heart, but it is the purpose of the Lord that prevails. (Proverbs 19:21 NIV)

Maggie continued, "I have been absolutely amazed at the goodness of God. He never ceases to amaze me. He seems to work best when I worry the least. He said one time that was one of the ways that I showed Him I trusted Him."

"I love this adventure we are on. It is so exciting. I feel like we are running up and down hills, just waiting to see what's on the other side, and it will be great surprises."

She continued, "He also said one time that because of Mark's and my speed, He had a special job for us on this ark. He said it won't be hard but that we must be ready to go and say what He says when He says to do it. He said that things will go much smoother if we do. I asked Him what was that, and He told me He would let me know when the time was right. I have a feeling it won't be too long."

In the meantime, Chuck was beginning to wonder how much longer they would be on this ark. He was getting a little anxious about being indoors for so long. He longed to see the sun and smell the fresh air. His thoughts were so strong that he accidentally spoke them out loud. "How much longer, God?" with a sound of desperation in his voice.

Noah's friend spoke and said, "Not much longer, I promise."

Chuck was flooded with a feeling of gratitude because he knew that God knew how he was feeling.

"I will soon be sending you a little messenger to tell you when you and all the other small animals can leave the ark."

And at this news, Chuck said, "Can I tell Lizzy?"

"Yes," replied God, "but not everyone else. I want this to be a smooth and uneventful exit, and leaving your new friends won't be easy for some."

Lizzy came around the corner and said in a very excited and happy voice, "Noah was seen letting out a bird today." She went on, "Gracie saw him doing it but was told by God not to go around telling everyone because it wasn't time yet. I happened to overhear Gracie telling Gilbert what she saw. She also said that she saw Noah look out, and he could see the top of some mountains.

Then he released the blackbird. She heard him tell Shem it was a raven."

Lizzy noticed an increased desire among those who knew this to spend more time with God and listen more to what He wanted to say, including herself. Her main question was, "God, when do we get to get off of this ark?"

The only reply at that time was, "Be patient, my dear one. More time is needed for water to dry up to make it safer for my creation."

Daily, all the animals that knew about the raven being let loose were pressing into more time with God—some out of fear and some out of being curious as to what God had planned for them when they were to get off the ark and find their own place in this new world. Many days passed, and the rumors started again about a white bird called a dove that was released. Although the blackbird never returned, the dove came back within a short few days. Noah waited seven days and then sent out the dove again. This time, she returned with a freshly picked leaf. It was a clear sign that vegetation was beginning to grow again and that the waters were receding.

Then God spoke to Mark and Maggie about their purpose for being on the ark. Because they could run so fast and get into so many tight places and out again, they were to be His message carriers to all the animals. The message was to start to get ready to leave the ark and that the large animals were to depart first and down in size until the very tiniest animals could leave the ark. He told them that Noah was going to wait seven days and then send out the dove again, but this time, she was not going to return. That was the sign that Noah would open the doors and lower the loading dock and that they could all start to depart. They were given strict orders to go at certain times to certain animal groups because God did not want a stampede. Even though there was great peace among all the animals, they were all getting very excited to see what their friend God had in store for them.

The animals that spent time with God seemed to be the ones that were the most excited about His plans for them. They were also the ones that were the least fearful and seemed to have more joy. When Lizzy and Chuck were in the presence of God, He told them which animals they were to travel with and where they were to go when they left the ark. He also started sharing with them the plans He had for humans far into the future. He told them that many generations from then, there would come a time when His son would come to the earth and save the humans who would believe in Him. But He added that is not for this time. He told them to be on the lookout for Mark and Maggie because when it was time to exit the ark, they had their instructions to get the animals to move toward the exit in an organized manner. The larger animals were to go first. Then each group after that would be smaller and smaller, being the last. God said, "It would be safer for all that way."

> You're off to great places, today is your day. Your mountain is waiting, so get on your way. (Dr. Seuss)

God told Chuck and Lizzy that many of the other animals had not spent much time with Him, so they would be confused and lack some direction. He asked if they could try to help some of them. Of course, they replied yes. God also said that the dove was not coming back and that Noah was waiting for a few more days to make sure.

Two more days went by, and just like God said, the dove did not come back. Mark was on standby close to Noah when he heard him tell his family to get the animals ready that they were going to get moving out. That was Mark's signal to get to the giraffes first, and Maggie went to the elephants and told them it was time to start lining up to exit. Then on to the next groups, they went just as God said to do it.

Slowly but very surely, the ark was emptied. As the animals left the ark, they gathered in groups that they were told by God to get into. Each group was instructed to go to a different part of the world that God said He already had prepared for them. He said just like He provided, protected, and planned for their journey to and on the ark, He would do for the rest of their lives as long as they stayed connected to Him.

About the Author

Maria Stanley is the mother of three and a total of sixteen (so far) grandchildren, grandchildren-in-law, and great-grandchildren (and still expecting many more to come—she hopes). She loves short story writing and illustrates all her own work. She is an artist living in Tulsa, who loves its spirit of creativity, which helps her continue to develop her skills. She stays busy with church and friends and paints as much as she can. She lives with her new friend Maggie.

www.ingramcontent.com/pod-product-compliance
Lightning Source LLC
LaVergne TN
LVHW060926090425
807896LV00033B/109
9798896370468